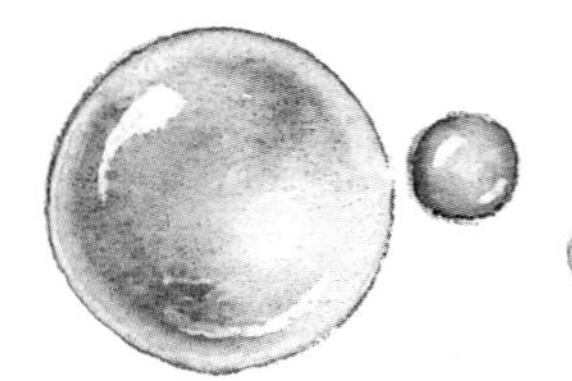

At Home with Science

Splish! Splosh!

Why do we wash?

Written by Janice Lobb
Illustrated by Peter Utton

KINGfISHER

KINGFISHER
Kingfisher Publications Plc
New Penderel House
283-288 High Holborn
London WC1V 7HZ

Contents

First published by Kingfisher Publications Plc 2000
10 9 8 7 6 5 4 3 2 1

ITR/1299/SC/FR(FR)/128MAWA

Created by Snapdragon Publishing Ltd

A CIP catalogue record for this book is available from the British Library.

ISBN 0 7534 0426 5

Printed in Hong Kong

Author Janice Lobb
Illustrators Peter Utton and Ann Savage (page 24)

For Snapdragon
Editorial Director Jackie Fortey
Art Director Chris Legee
Designer Richard Rowan

For Kingfisher
Series Editor Camilla Reid
Series Art Editor Mike Buckley
DTP Co-ordinator Nicky Studdart
Production Kelly Johnson

About this book

Lying back in a hot, bubbly bath doesn't feel like science, does it? Well it is! So is brushing your teeth, drying yourself ... and even flushing the toilet! This book is about the science that is happening around you, every day, in your bathroom. Keep your eyes open and you'll be surprised at what you discover!

Hall of Fame

Archie and his friends are here to help you. They are each named after famous scientists – apart from Bob the duck, who is a young scientist just like you!

Archie

ARCHIMEDES (287–212BC)
The Greek scientist Archimedes worked out why things float or sink while in the bath. According to the story, he was so pleased that he leapt out, shouting "Eureka!", which means "I've done it!".

Frank

BENJAMIN FRANKLIN (1706–1790)
This American statesman carried out a famous (but dangerous) experiment in 1752. By flying a kite in a storm he showed that a flash of lightning was electricity. This helped people to protect buildings during storms.

Marie

MARIE CURIE (1867–1934)
Girls did not go to university in Poland, where Marie Curie grew up, so she went to study in Paris, France. She worked on radioactivity and received two Nobel prizes for her discoveries, in 1903 and 1911.

Dot

DOROTHY HODGKIN (1910–1994)
Dorothy Hodgkin was a British scientist who made many important discoveries about molecules and atoms, the tiny particles that make up everything around us. She was given the Nobel prize for Chemistry in 1964.

See for yourself!

1 Read about the science in your bathroom, then try the 'See for yourself!' experiments to discover how it works. In science, experiments try to find or show the answers.

2 Carefully read the instructions for each experiment, making sure you follow the numbered steps in the correct order.

3 Here are some of the things you will need. Have everything ready before you start each experiment.

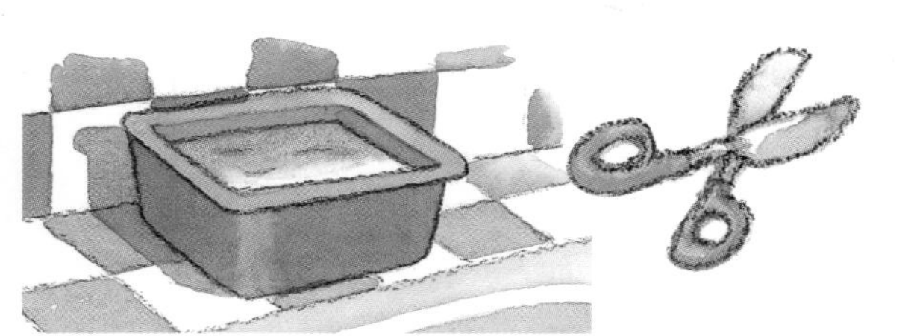

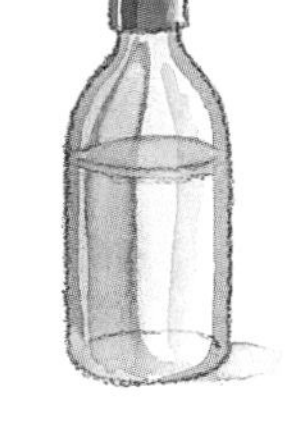

Plastic tub

Scissors

Plastic bottle

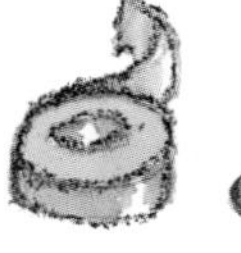

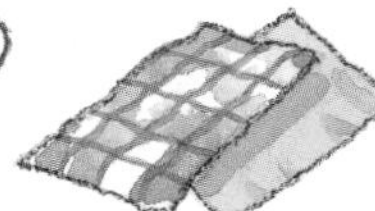

Sticky tape

Spoon

Fabric scraps

Glass bowl

4 Safety first!

Some scientists take risks to make their discoveries, but our experiments are safe. Just make sure that you tell an adult what you are doing and get their help when you see the red warning button.

Amazing facts

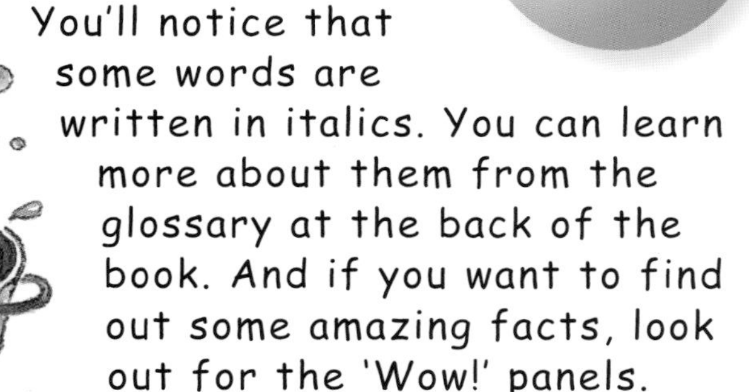

You'll notice that some words are written in italics. You can learn more about them from the glossary at the back of the book. And if you want to find out some amazing facts, look out for the 'Wow!' panels.

What is a wave?

A wave is simply *energy* moving from one place to another. Sometimes we can see waves, like those that move through water. Other waves, such as sound waves, are invisible because they travel through air. A wave does not happen by itself – something has to start it off. We call this a *disturbance*.

As the energy passes through the water, it moves the water up and down.

The water doesn't move forward with the wave, so Bob just bobs up and down in the same place.

See for yourself!

1 Make your own bathtime waves by tapping the surface of the water. Try a gentle tap, followed by a big one. What do you see?

2 Give the water several quick taps. You should find that this makes waves with crests that are close together. Now try tapping slowly.

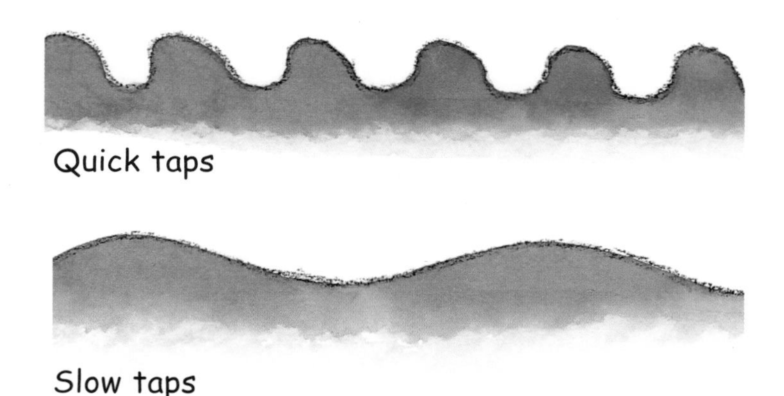

Quick taps

Slow taps

3 What happens when a wave reaches the side of the bath? It doesn't disappear but bounces off and comes back. This is called *reflection*.

Giant ocean waves

Ocean waves are caused by the wind. A gentle wind makes small waves, while strong winds whip up big, high waves. Sometimes, when an earthquake happens under the sea, a huge wave called a tsunami is created. A tsunami can be over 30 metres tall when it reaches the shore. This sort of wave can be very dangerous.

How does soap get me clean?

Your skin produces oil to keep itself smooth and stretchy. But when you get dirt on your skin, the dirt sticks to this oil and plain water will not wash it off. This is because oil and water do not mix, so the water just rolls off the oily, dirty skin. Soap gets your skin clean because it acts as a *detergent*.

What did the soap say to the bubbles?

Don't forget to foam!

Soap in action

A detergent works by mixing the oil and water together.

The soap breaks the dirty oil up into little droplets and holds it in the water. This mixture is called an *emulsion*.

With the dirt and oil removed from your skin, you are left nice and clean!

See for yourself!

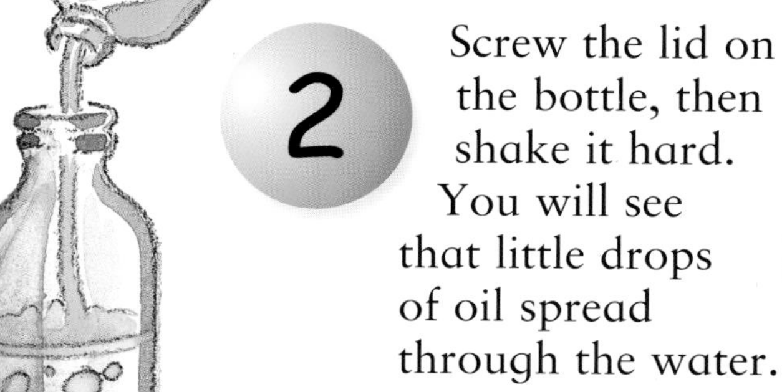

1 Half fill a small clear plastic bottle (about 300 millilitres in size) with water, then add a thin layer of cooking oil. Hold the bottle up to the light and look through the side. Do the oil and water mix?

2 Screw the lid on the bottle, then shake it hard. You will see that little drops of oil spread through the water.

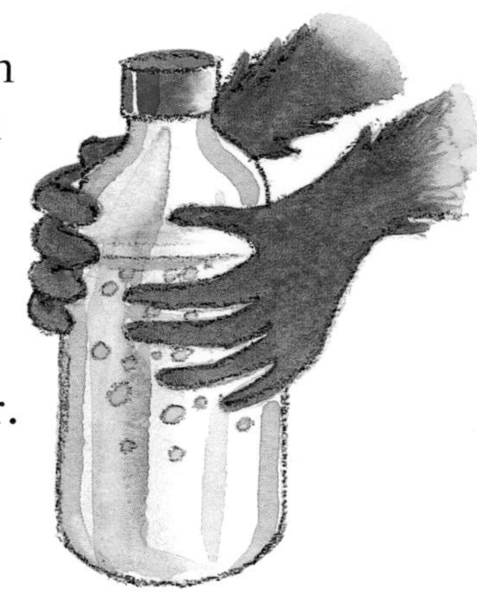

3 Stop shaking and leave the mixture for a couple of minutes. Watch what happens to the oil and water. How have the droplets of oil changed?

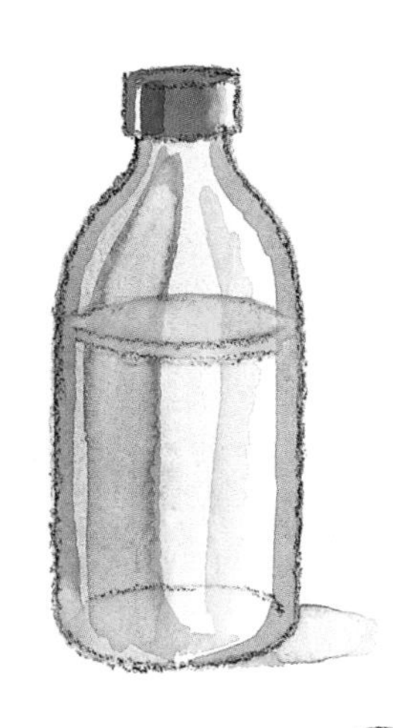

4 Now add a squirt of shampoo to the bottle, put the lid on and shake it up again. The water stays cloudy because the shampoo has mixed the oil and water in an emulsion.

Sticky scum

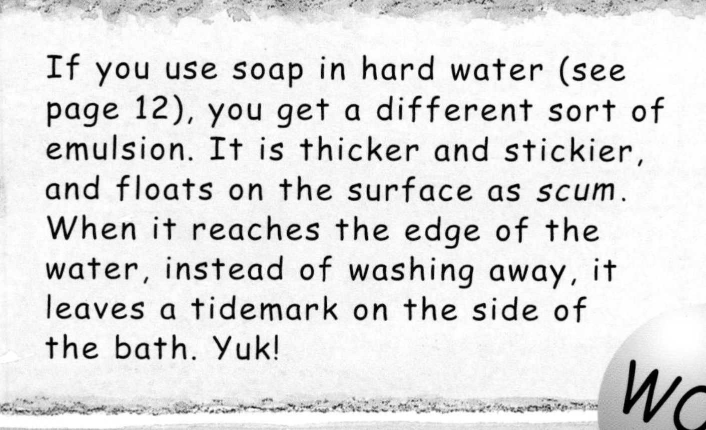

If you use soap in hard water (see page 12), you get a different sort of emulsion. It is thicker and stickier, and floats on the surface as *scum*. When it reaches the edge of the water, instead of washing away, it leaves a tidemark on the side of the bath. Yuk!

WOW!

Why does a toy boat float?

Have you noticed that some things float but others sink? Whether an object floats or sinks depends on how heavy it is and what size it is. Together, these two things make the object's *density*. Anything more dense than water sinks to the bottom of the bath. Air is less dense than water, so it always floats. A toy boat floats because it is hollow and the air inside it makes it float. Bob floats for the same reason – but Archie sinks!

What sinks?

Test some of these objects to see which ones float and which sink.

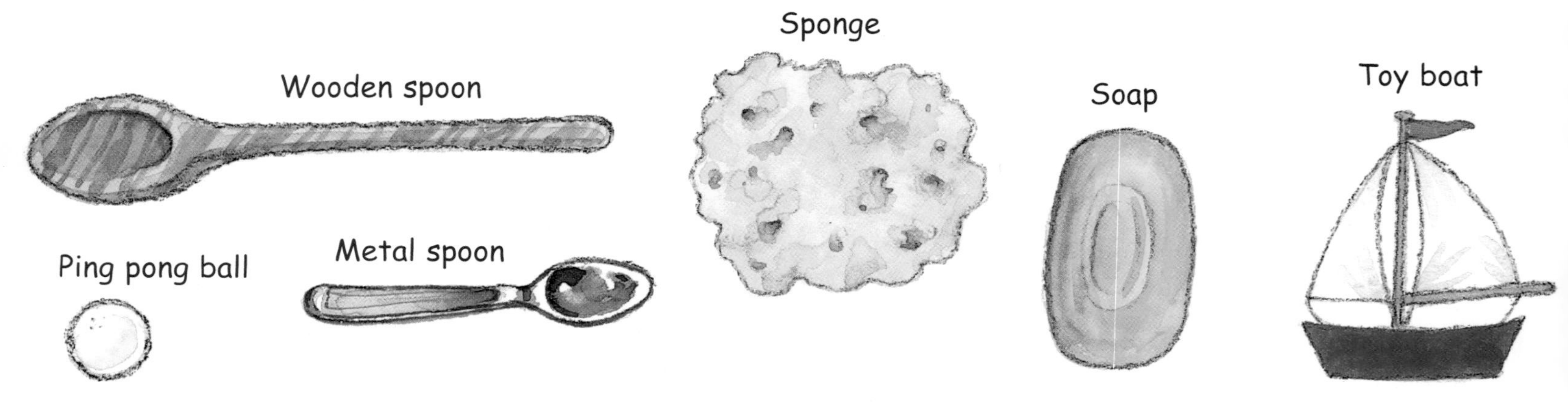

See for yourself!

Hollow objects float because the air inside them makes their overall density less than the density of water. A plastic cup is more dense than water but, with air inside it, it floats.

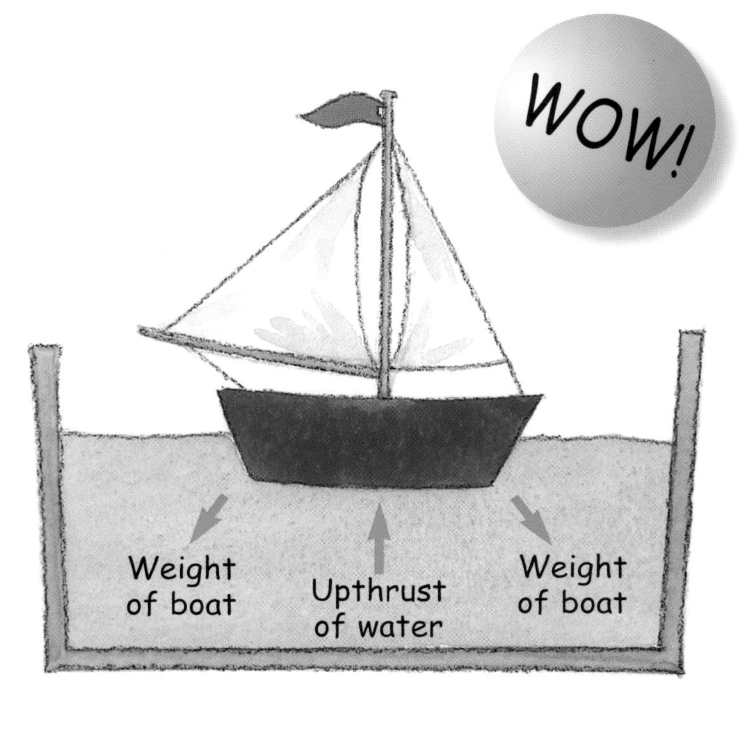

1 Take a clear plastic cup and put it in the bath upside down. As you push it down, notice that no water enters the cup.

2 Keep pushing down until the cup is under the water. Does it get harder to push down? Now try tipping the cup slightly. Do you see air bubbles escaping?

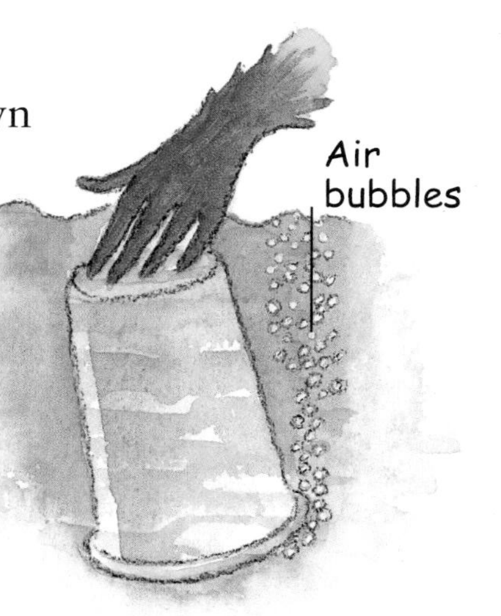

3 With the air gone from inside it, the cup is denser than water and so it sinks.

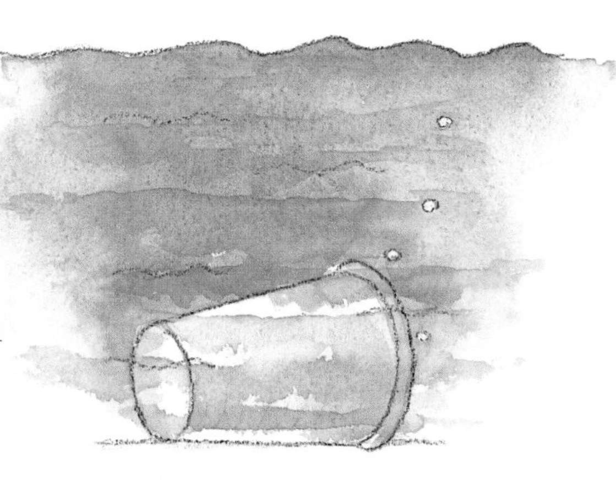

Water forces

When a boat is put into water, the water pushes against it with a force called *upthrust*. If the weight of the boat is less than the force of the upthrust, then the boat stays afloat. If the weight of the boat is greater than the upthrust then the boat will sink.

What is hard water?

All water may look the same, but did you know that some water is *hard* and other water is *soft*? Hard water is found in places where there are chalk or limestone rocks under the ground. Rainwater flows over these rocks and picks up tiny particles of *calcium*. This is carried by the water and we say it has become 'hard'. Pure rainwater has no calcium in it and we call it 'soft' water.

Blowing bubbles

Get your hands soapy, make a big O with your finger and thumb, then try to blow a bubble!

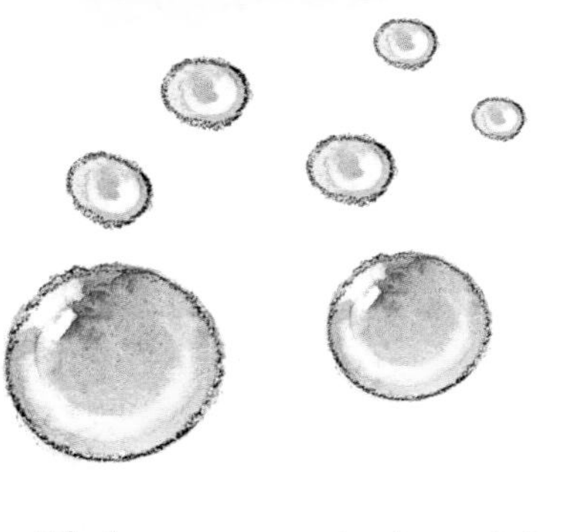

If the water is hard it will be difficult to make bubbles with soap. It also makes a ring of scum around the edge of the bath.

See for yourself!

1 Half fill a jar with soft water, such as rainwater. Add a small piece of soap and shake the jar. How much froth does it make?

2 Now make your own hard water by putting a piece of chalk in another jar, this time filled with fizzy water. Wait for the chalk to dissolve.

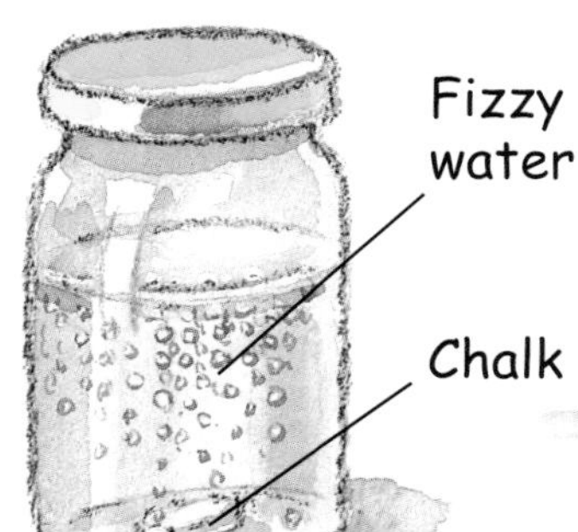

3 Put a piece of soap into this chalky, hard water and shake it up. Do you see bubbles or scum? You should see scum.

4 Finally, shake up some soap in a jar of your home tap water. Is it hard or soft?

If you see bubbles, your water is soft. If you see scum, you have hard water

Scaly shower

WOW!

When hard water is heated, the calcium it is carrying comes out of the water again. You can see this as *limescale* on the inside of a kettle. Limescale can also block up the holes in your shower and stop it from working.

Calcium in hard water helps to give you strong teeth and bones!

Why do I go red in the bath?

When you get into a hot bath, the *nerves* in your skin tell your body that it is getting warm. To stop you overheating, your body starts to cool itself by bringing the blood to the surface of the skin, where it can give off heat. If your skin looks red, or flushed, it is because you can see this blood just under the surface. In hot weather, or when you have a temperature, you go red for the same reason.

Tiny tubes

Your blood flows through tiny tubes called *capillaries*. If they have blood in them your skin is hot. If they are empty your skin is cold.

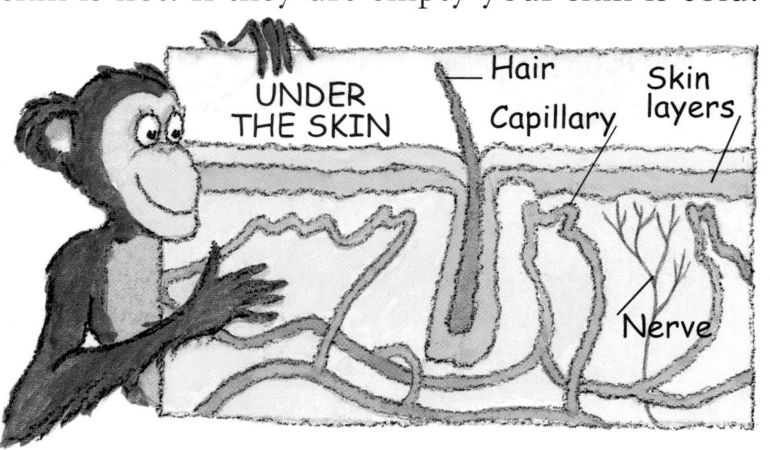

Animals in hot countries need to keep cool too. Although elephants do not go red, they have big ears with a large area of skin which helps them to lose heat.

See for yourself!

1 Line up three bowls. Put ice-cold water into one, warm water into the second and very warm water into the third.

Ice-cold water

Warm water

Very warm water

2 Ask an adult to check that the very warm water is not too hot to touch. It should feel like very warm bath water.

Very warm water

3 Put one hand in the cold water and your other hand in the very warm water. Now move both hands into the warm water.

Cold water

Very warm water

4 Your two hands feel very different because, at first, the nerves can only tell you that there have been changes in temperature. Eventually, they adjust to the new temperature.

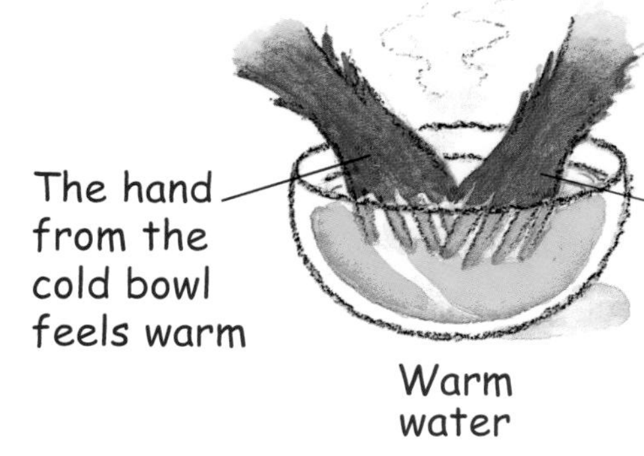

Red for go!

WOW!

Blood gets its colour from a red substance called *haemoglobin*. This carries oxygen around the body to give us energy. It is the mineral iron which makes the haemoglobin red. Amazingly, your body contains enough iron to make a nail!

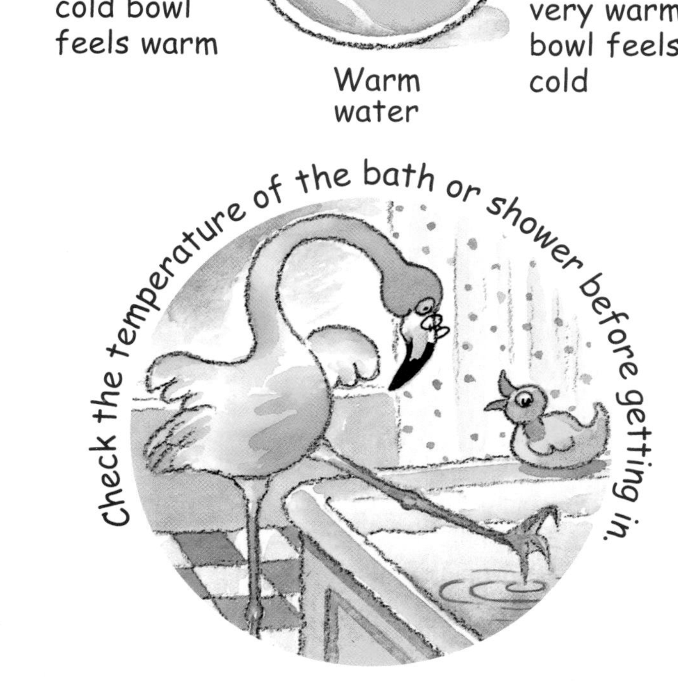

What makes a shower work?

Flowing water is pushed along by the force of the water behind it. This force is called *water pressure*. When water comes out of a tap it stays together as a single stream, but in a shower the water has to come out of lots of tiny holes. Forcing the same amount of water out of small holes increases the water pressure and gives you lots of little jets of water. And because the holes in a shower head are all at a slightly different angles, the water spreads out in different directions.

Feel the pressure

If you stand close to the shower head, you can feel the water pressure.

Frank's shower has an electric pump to help push the water along and out. Bob's has a tank above his shower. The water is pushed out by the pressure of the water in the tank above.

See for yourself!

1 Find an empty plastic drinks bottle and ask an adult to make a line of four holes from top to bottom (see page 32 for method). This is tricky, so don't try to do this by yourself.

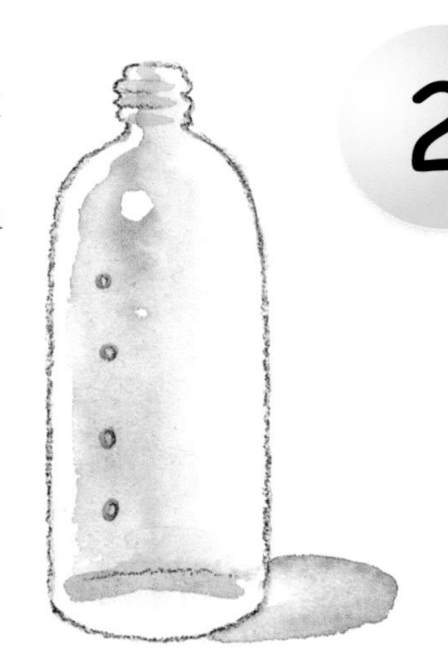

2 When you are in the bath, fill the bottle with bath water and stand it on a bath rack or on the side of the bath.

3 The water pressure is greatest at the bottom of the bottle so the lowest jet travels furthest.

4 As the water runs out, the pressure falls and the jets get smaller. This is why you don't get a good shower if you have low water pressure in your house.

Superjets

When water is forced out through a small hole it travels further than if it is pushed through a larger one. You can try this with a garden hose by putting your finger over the hole at the end. How far you can make the water travel?

Why does bath water go cold?

If you have ever stayed in a bath for a long time, you will know that the bath soon cools down and you start to feel rather chilly. This is because of a process called *evaporation*. Over time, some of the surface water has escaped into the air as tiny *particles* called *water vapour*. As this water evaporates, it takes the heat from the bath with it into the colder bathroom air, cooling down the water and warming up the bathroom.

Why do mirrors mist up?

Invisible water vapour hits a cold mirror...

...and turns back into drops of liquid water.

Feel the wetness on the mirror. This is called *condensation*.

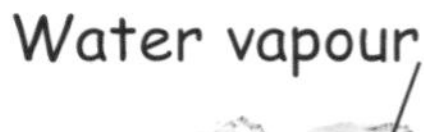

See for yourself!

1 Dry one of your hands and wet the other in the bath.

2 Hold your two index fingers in front of your mouth and blow on them.

3 As the water evaporates from your wet finger, it takes the heat from your finger with it, making it feel colder. The longer you blow, the colder it feels. Your dry finger does not feel as cold.

4 Hold your fingers against your face. Do they feel different?

Your dry finger will feel quite warm

Your wet finger should feel much colder

Full steam ahead!

WOW!

Steam is hot water vapour that comes from water when it boils (at 100°C). We see steam when it condenses in the air. Steam can be useful – a steam iron is very good at getting the creases out of clothes.

Why must I brush my teeth?

Although teeth are hard, they are actually living things, and grow from the jawbone out through the gums. *Milk teeth* grow first when we are babies. Then, as we get older, they fall out and are replaced by adult teeth. After that, we do not grow any more teeth so it is important to look after them. Brushing keeps them white and healthy.

Different kinds of teeth

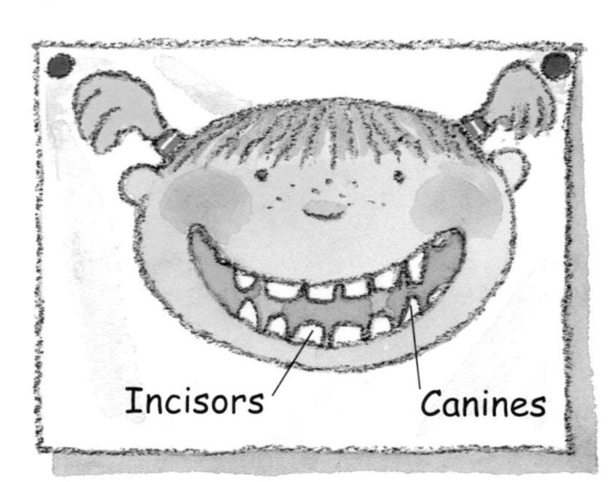

Front teeth, called incisors, are for cutting and nibbling food. Canines are pointed teeth for tearing food.

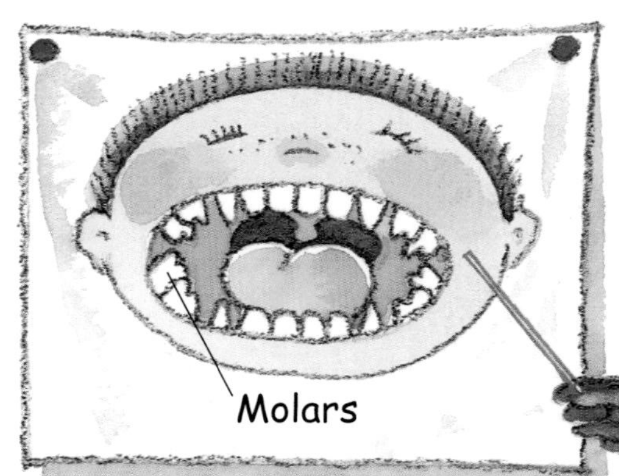

The teeth at the back of the mouth are called molars. They are for grinding up large pieces of food.

The shiny white surface of the tooth is hard *enamel*. It protects the tooth and gives it sharp cutting edges

See for yourself!

1 How many teeth do you have? If you have not lost any yet, you will probably have 20 milk teeth. Adults have 32 teeth.

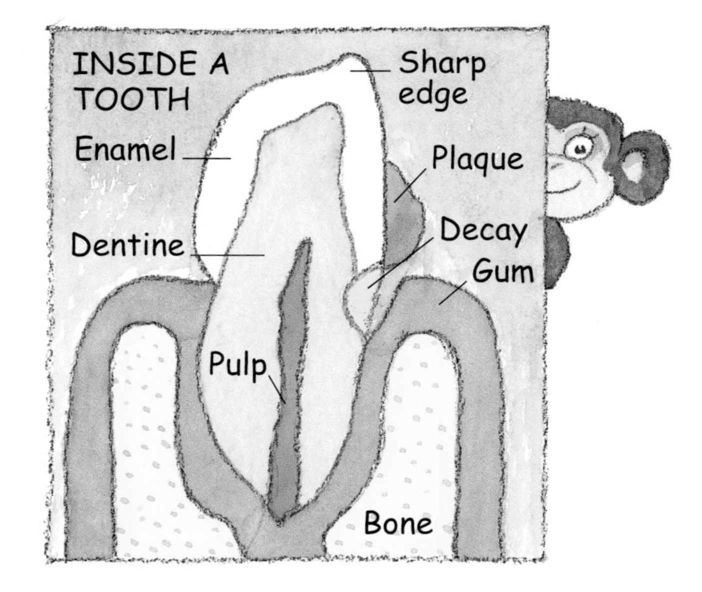

2 When one of your milk teeth falls out, have a careful look at it. It is hollow underneath, where the blood vessels kept it alive, and has shiny white enamel on top.

Plaque attack!

WOW!

A tooth has three layers – soft pulp at the centre, a hard layer of dentine in the middle, and a tough coating of enamel on the outside. Without brushing, a layer of *plaque* forms on your teeth. Eventually this hardens and starts to make acids which attack your teeth and gums. If this happens, you will need a filling.

3 Put your tooth in a glass of cola and leave it for several days. As the sugary acid attacks the tooth you will see that it starts to go brown and decay.

How does a towel get me dry?

Materials like towels are *porous*, which means they *absorb*, or soak up, water easily. If you look closely at a dry towel you will see that it is made of a woven cotton material which is covered with little loops. These loops are like tiny pockets full of air. When you wrap yourself in the towel, the water is drawn into the loops and the air is pushed out. So the towel gets wet – and you get dry!

Why doesn't Bob get wet?

Bob doesn't get wet because he's *waterproof*, which means that he cannot absorb water. Instead, the water forms droplets on his surface, then runs off. If you drop water onto your hand you'll see that you are waterproof too. That's why you don't get soggy in the bath!

See for yourself!

1 Collect some different materials, such as an old towel, cotton or wool fabric, newspaper, a piece of cotton wool and a plastic bag.

2 Cut them into strips about 10 centimetres long and fix them with strong sticky tape to a plastic ruler. Support the ruler over a bowl of water, with all the pieces just touching the water.

3 Watch each strip to see what happens to the water. Which one soaks up the most water?

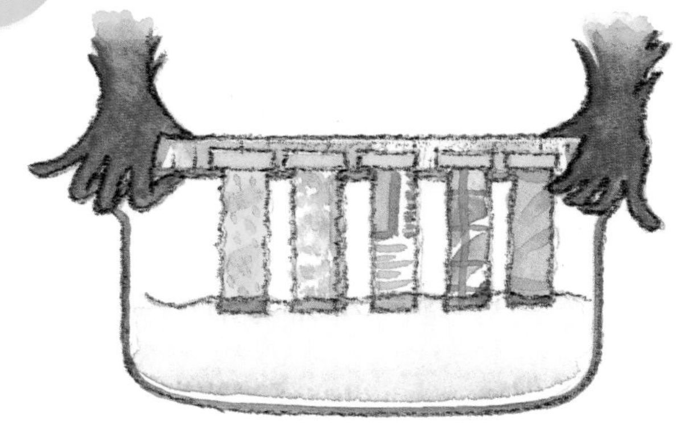

WOW!

Squeezy skeletons

Sponges are porous because they are full of holes which can soak up lots of water. A natural sponge is the soft skeleton of a creature which once lived under the sea. Sponges are collected in warm seas by divers, or pulled into boats with hooks. Most people today use artificial sponges.

How does the toilet flush?

When you turn the handle on the *cistern* of a toilet, it begins something called a *siphon* effect. This starts water flowing from the cistern into the toilet bowl. Although the water always wants to flow from the cistern to the bowl, it can't because a bent pipe blocks its way. By activating the siphon, water can flow up this pipe, then down to the bowl.

Inside a toilet

As the handle goes down, a lever inside pulls up the disc. One side of the pipe fills with water and pushes the air out of the way.

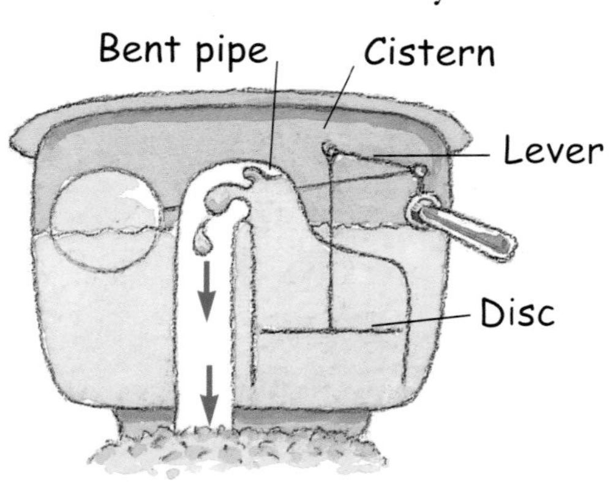

When the water gets up to the bend at the top of the siphon, it starts to flow down the other side of the pipe.

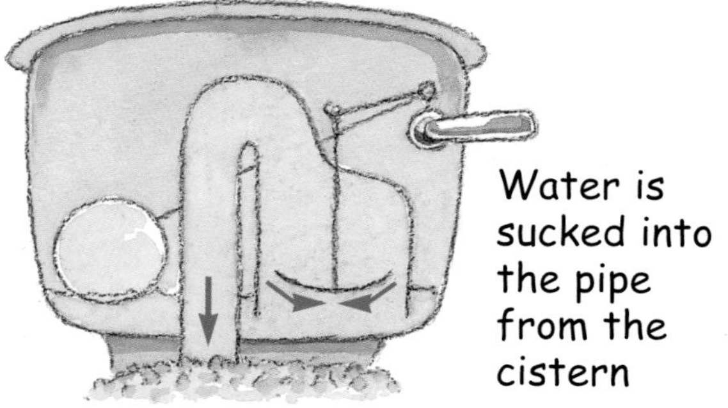

Once the water has started flowing, it can't stop until the cistern is empty. Then the cistern fills up, ready to flush again.

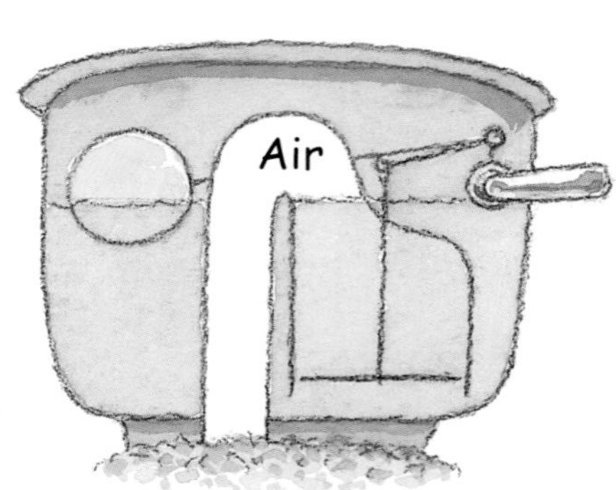

See for yourself!

1 To find out how a siphon works, first fill a plastic tub with water then stand it on the edge of a bath full of water.

2 Put one end of a piece of plastic tubing in the tub and the other end in the bath. Air is trapped in the tubing so water cannot flow through it.

3 Now put the whole of the tubing under the bath water and fill it up. Cover one end of the tubing with your thumb and put it back in the tub. Keep the other end in the bath.

Make sure there are no air bubbles in the tube

4 Now take your thumb away. See the water go! Because there is no air between the two water levels, the water is siphoned out and the tub empties.

The first flush!

WOW!

The flush toilet was invented by Sir John Harington in about 1591. He built one for Queen Elizabeth I at her palace in Richmond, Surrey. In those days a toilet was called a jakes or a privy. Other names we use today are the lavatory and W.C., which is short for watercloset.

What is the bath made of?

Most baths look alike, but some are made from iron, some are made of *steel* and others are made of *plastic*. A bath made of iron doesn't look as though it is made of metal because it is coated with a layer of glassy enamel. Other things in the bathroom made of iron may be covered in paint or *chrome* to stop them from rusting.

The magnet test

Use a magnet to find out what material your bath is made of. If it is iron or steel, the magnet will stick. The enamel on the surface will not stop it from working.

If the bath is plastic, the magnet will fall off. See what else in the bathroom attracts the magnet. Are your water pipes or radiators made of iron?

See for yourself!

1 Find out what materials things are made of by touch alone. Hold a plastic object, such as a beaker. It should feel warm.

A beaker feels warm because plastic is a poor conductor of heat

2 When you touch metal objects, they feel cold. Unlike plastic, metal takes heat away from your hand quickly. It is a good *conductor* of heat.

An iron bath feels cold

3 Touch other materials in your bathroom. What are they made of? Do they feel warm or cold?

4 Which materials are natural (like wood) and which are made (like steel, glass and plastic)?

Hip, hip, hooray!

WOW!

Before houses had bathrooms, people took hip baths in their bedrooms. A hip bath was usually made of iron and had no taps or plughole. The water had to be carried to the bath in a bucket. It was quite cosy having a bath in your bedroom in front of a roaring fire.

Remember baths and taps need to be kept clean!

What can I see in the mirror?

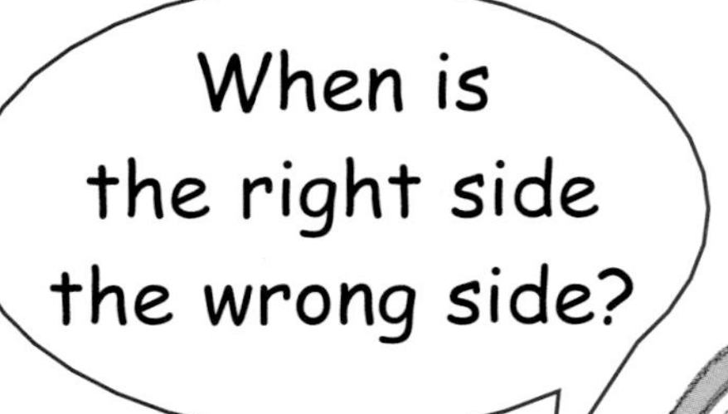

What you see when you look in a mirror is not yourself, but a reflection or *mirror image* of yourself. Strange as it may seem, you don't see yourself as other people see you. They see you the 'right' way round. If you look at your reflection and a photo of yourself at the same time, you will see the difference.

When you look in a mirror!

Bouncing light!

Without light, we cannot see anything. We see an object because light travels from a source (the Sun or, as shown here, a torch), bounces off the object and then comes to our eyes.

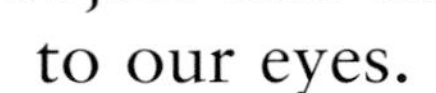

Light rays bounce off the mirror

Light rays travel in straight lines

When light bounces off a smooth, shiny surface more of it bounces back to you than from other objects. This is why you see a reflection.

See for yourself!

1

Stand close to a mirror, so that you can touch it. Then move it as far away as you can. The image moves too.

2

Stay still for a minute and look at your image.

It will seem to be the same distance behind the mirror as you are in front of it.

3

Wave your left hand. Which hand is the image waving? Is it the right or the left?

Funfair mirrors can do peculiar things to your reflection! Look at yourself in both sides of a spoon. Does it have to curve outwards or inwards to make you look smaller?

Bathroom quiz

1. What is the highest part of a wave called?
   a) A crust
   b) A crest
   c) A trough

2. What is formed when you mix soap, oil and water together?
   a) An emulsion
   b) An illusion
   c) A detergent

3. What substance does hard water contain that soft water does not?
   a) Air
   b) Soap
   c) Calcium

4. What happens when water vapour hits a cold surface?
   a) It condenses
   b) It evaporates
   c) Nothing

5. Which kind of teeth are used for nibbling?
   a) Incisors
   b) Molars
   c) Canines

6. Water is pushed through the holes of a shower by what?
   a) Water vapour
   b) Water pressure
   c) Upthrust

7. Materials that absorb water are described as being what?
   a) Waterproof
   b) Plastic
   c) Porous

8. Which of these substances will a magnet stick to?
   a) Iron
   b) Plastic
   c) Marble

9. What is the name for the tiny tubes that carry blood under the skin?
   a) Nerves
   b) Hairs
   c) Capillaries

10. When light bounces off a mirror, what happens to it?
    a) It is absorbed
    b) It is reflected
    c) It condenses

Answers on page 32

Glossary

Absorb
To soak up a liquid.

Calcium
Mineral found in rocks such as chalk and limestone.

Capillaries
Smallest of all the vessels which carry blood, forming fine networks under the skin surface.

Chrome (or chromium)
Expensive metal used to coat other cheaper metals, such as iron, to prevent them from rusting.

Cistern
Storage tank of the toilet for holding water.

Condensation
Water that has changed from an invisible vapour to a visible liquid.

Conductor
Material which transfers heat, but doesn't itself move.

Density
The amount of a substance contained within a certain space.

Detergent
A substance which stops the oil and water in an emulsion from separating into layers.

Disturbance
Movement of something from its original position, giving out energy.

Emulsion
A mixture of droplets of one type of liquid in another liquid.

Enamel
Hard, shiny substance.

Energy
The ability to do work (make things happen).

Evaporation
When water turns from being visible liquid to being invisible water vapour.

Haemoglobin
A substance found in the blood which contains iron, and is needed to carry oxygen around the body.

Hard water
Water which will not lather with soap because it contains calcium.

Limescale
Solid chalky material which comes out of hard water when it is heated.

Milk teeth
Small first teeth in mammals (like us!) which fall out and are replaced by larger adult teeth.

Mirror image
Picture made by a reflection in a shiny surface.

Nerve
Fibre in the body which carries messages from your senses to the brain, and gives instructions to your muscles.

Particles
Very small pieces of something.

Plastic
Manufactured material, made from the chemicals in oil, which can be moulded into any shape.

Plaque
Build-up of bacteria which stick to the teeth and cause tooth decay.

Porous
Full of tiny holes which are filled with air and so can take up liquids, such as water.

Reflection
Bouncing of light or water waves back off a surface.

Scum
Thick emulsion of dirt, water and oil, formed when trying to wash with soap in hard water.

Siphon
A bent tube that allows water to be drawn from a high point to a lower level.

Soft water
Water, such as rain-water, with no calcium and magnesium salts dissolved in it.

Steel
A strong, shiny metal that is a mix of iron and other metals.

Upthrust
The upwards push of water which helps objects to float.

Water pressure
A push moving through a body of water, when it is squeezed from outside.

Waterproof
Not letting liquid water pass through it.

Water vapour
Free water particles, moving around in the air, after water has evaporated.

Index

Answers to the Bathroom quiz on page 30
1 b 2 a 3 c 4 a 5 a 6 b 7 c 8 a 9 c 10 b

For adults only: to make a hole in a plastic bottle, heat the end of a skewer in a flame before piercing the side of the bottle.